RACISM

Essential Issues

RACISM

BY A. M. BUCKLEY

Content Consultant
Eileen O'Brien, PhD
Department of Sociology & Anthropology
Christopher Newport University

ABDO
Publishing Company

CREDITS

Published by ABDO Publishing Company, 8000 West 78th Street, Edina, Minnesota 55439. Copyright © 2011 by Abdo Consulting Group, Inc. International copyrights reserved in all countries. No part of this book may be reproduced in any form without written permission from the publisher. The Essential Library™ is a trademark and logo of ABDO Publishing Company.

Printed in the United States of America, North Mankato, Minnesota
112010
012011

 THIS BOOK CONTAINS AT LEAST 10% RECYCLED MATERIALS.

Editor: Rebecca Rowell
Copy Editor: Paula Lewis
Interior Design and Production: Marie Tupy
Cover Design: Marie Tupy

Library of Congress Cataloging-in-Publication Data
Buckley, A. M., 1968-
  Racism / by A. M. Buckley.
    p. cm. -- (Essential issues)
  Includes bibliographical references.
  ISBN 978-1-61714-777-7
  1. Los Angeles (Calif.)--Race relations--Juvenile literature.
  2. Minorities--California--Los Angeles--Juvenile literature. 3. Racism--California--Los Angeles--Juvenile literature. 4. Riots--California--Los Angeles--Juvenile literature. I. Title. II. Series.

  E184.A1B8983 2011
  305.8009794'94--dc22

                    2010044650

TABLE OF CONTENTS

*Video shot by George Holliday of police officers
beating Rodney King highlighted the issue of racism in the United States.*

A City in Flames

On March 3, 1991, Rodney King, a
25-year-old African-American man, was
caught speeding in South Los Angeles. When King
stepped out of his car after being pulled over by the
police, four white officers beat and kicked him while

17 other officers looked on. King suffered multiple skull fractures and damage to his brain and kidney from the attack.

George Holliday, a white resident in a nearby apartment building, captured the scene with his camcorder. Dismayed by what he saw, Holliday gave the video to a local television station. The tape promptly aired on television stations around the world. Millions of people were horrified by what they saw as police brutality.

The Los Angeles Police Department also received a copy of the tape. The four officers who beat King were charged with assault with a deadly weapon and the use of excessive force. While waiting for their trial to begin, three of the officers—veterans of the force— were suspended from duty. The fourth, a probationary officer, was fired. Because King was African American and the officers were white, the incident brought renewed attention to the long and troubled history with race and racism in the United States.

Five Days of Fire

In April 1992, the four police officers who beat King were tried in court. The trial took place in Simi Valley, a mostly white area of Los Angeles where many police officers lived. On April 29, the all-white jury made its decision. Three of the officers were found not guilty. The fourth, Laurence Powell, was found guilty of using excessive force. The judge immediately overturned the guilty ruling, and all four officers were free of charges.

To many, the trial seemed unfair from the outset. King became a symbol of the bias, oppression, and unjust conditions that persisted in cities and towns across the United States as a result

Changing Minority

The idea that people of color are a minority in the United States is changing. At the beginning of the twenty-first century, California became the first state in which whites were no longer a majority of the population. According to a 2008 report by the US Census Bureau, there will be more Americans who collectively identify themselves as Hispanic, black or African American, Asian, American Indian, native Hawaiian, or Pacific Islander than non-Hispanic whites by 2042.

Majority can be thought of in different ways. In addition to referring to more than half of a group, the term also refers to a group's share of power and resources in the society. So, while the number of people of color in California may now be greater than the number of whites, the people of color will need to have equal or greater power and resources to truly no longer be the minority. This includes equal political representation, an equal share of wealth and property, and equal life chances such as life expectancy, levels of education, and employment. For example, in the United States, African-American unemployment is often twice that of white unemployment, which challenges the idea that whites are no longer the majority. If African Americans had an equal share of opportunities, there would not be such disparity in the unemployment levels between whites and African Americans.

of institutional racism. This occurs when the structures, policies, or laws of a society or organization—including a government—are based on racist ideas. Rather than treating all groups equally, they create inequality between groups, including races.

Many Angelenos—the people of Los Angeles—who watched the verdicts on television had strong reactions. Thousands flocked to Parker Center, the police headquarters downtown, for what began as a peaceful protest. As night fell, some of the protesters smashed car windshields and set trees and cars aflame.

Types of Protest

The rioting that took place in Los Angeles in 1992 was a type of protest. It is one of several ways an individual or a group can take action in support of a belief or cause. Other types of protest include sit-ins, marches, boycotts, and taking legal action. Civil rights activists used a variety of protests to bring attention to the issue of racism and discrimination in the United States. But they were not the first Americans to use such tactics. The Boston Tea Party in December 1773 was a protest by colonists against actions taken by the British Parliament regarding tea, including a tax.

In South Los Angeles, at the corner of Florence and Normandie Avenues, where King had been beaten, violence broke out quickly. A white man was pulled from his truck by a group of African-American men and brutally assaulted. An angry mob attacked a Guatemalan immigrant as he stepped off a city bus until an African-American man escorted him to safety. A Chinese-American man was taken from his car, beaten, and robbed. In South Los Angeles, and in the central city, people set stores on fire. Some threw bottles and rocks. People of all ages and races stole food, furniture, diapers, appliances—anything they could take—from burnt-out stores. The police were rarely visible in the streets during these early hours of rioting.

People rioted and Los Angeles burned. Streets were filled with noise and fire, violence and looting. On the third day, 10,000 California National Guard troops, 2,000 soldiers from the US Army, and 1,500 members of the US Marine Corps arrived to try to stop the riots. By May 4, more than 50 people had been killed, and more than 2,000 had been hospitalized for their injuries. More than 12,000 people had been arrested. Property damage was severe, totaling more than $800 million.

"People, I just want to say, you know, can we all get along? Can we get along? Can we stop making it, making it horrible for the older people and the kids? . . . Please, we can get along here. We all can get along. I mean, we're all stuck here for a while. Let's try to work it out. Let's try to beat it. Let's try to beat it. Let's try to work it out."[1]
—*Rodney King, May 1, 1992*

What Is Racism?

Riots, also called civil disturbances, occur when a group of people erupts in anger and takes to the streets. Several major US cities other than Los Angeles have experienced race riots. These include Washington DC, Chicago, Detroit, and New York. People worldwide have also rioted, including citizens in Australia, South Africa, and France. There is not one simple reason for why riots take place. They usually begin as a response to one incident, but the anger expressed by rioters often has been brewing for decades. Rioting is one response to the injustice and oppression that results from racism.

To discriminate against a person based on skin color is racist. Racism also includes believing one race is better than another. Direct racism can take the form of name-calling, withholding freedoms, degrading treatment, and physical assault. Racism can also be expressed in subtle ways through economics, politics,

King Renewed Hope

As recently as the 1960s, African Americans could not testify in court on their own behalf. This often meant the police could harass or attack African Americans without recourse. When Holliday, a white man, caught the King beating on video, it seemed that this long-standing pattern would begin to change. But that hope was lost when the officers were found not guilty in the King trial. The sense of hopelessness and inability to obtain justice through legal and peaceful means resulted in lawlessness because people no longer had a reason to trust or believe in the social structure to solve their problems.

Rioting as Protest

In the book *Poor People's Movements: Why They Succeed, How They Fail*, Frances Fox Piven and Richard Clowards examined rioting. History shows it has reaped political results. Under the right political conditions, rioting is a prudent strategy for obtaining concessions from the state. The authors explained, "As the numbers of blacks in the cities grew [in the first half of the twentieth century], their protests began to produce concessions from political leaders. Each concession . . . conferred legitimacy on the goals of the struggle and gave reason for hope that the goals could be reached, with the result that protest was stimulated all the more."[2]

and the distribution of resources. Racism can occur between individuals or, more broadly, by institutions. To understand racism, it is important to explore what racism means, who perpetrates it, where it comes from, and how it occurs in the United States.

African Americans have suffered profound racism in the United States. Other ethnic groups have experienced racism as well, including Native Americans, Asian Americans, Latinos, and Arab Americans. Whites have held most of the power in the United States for more than three centuries. But a difference in treatment of one race by another occurred well before the United States was officially a nation. ⸺

People marched between burned buildings
in Los Angeles during the riots in 1992.

*Columbus's kind welcome by natives in the New World
was not returned by the explorer and his crew.*

RACISM
IN THE UNITED STATES

he roots of racism in the United States
lie overseas more than 500 years ago.
Christopher Columbus arrived in the Bahamas,
in North America, in 1492. The native Arawak
people greeted the explorer and his crew generously,

bringing "parrots and balls of cotton and spears and many other things."[1] Their kindness was not returned. The Europeans wanted to expand their resources and territories. As a result, they killed the majority of the indigenous peoples they encountered in the Caribbean islands. By 1550, only 500 remained.

The Europeans' treatment of the indigenous peoples had the superiority of racism. Columbus wrote in his log, "With fifty men we could subjugate them all and make them do whatever we want."[2] Rather than accept the people they encountered, with their unique customs and distinct physical characteristics, Columbus and his crew instead chose violent separation and conquest.

This set the stage for subsequent travelers to North America. The Europeans who later journeyed to and settled what is now the United

A New Look at History

Howard Zinn's *A People's History of the United States: 1492–Present* was first published in 1980. Zinn's book presented for the first time a comprehensive history of the nation from the point of view of those who had been exploited or discriminated against in the march toward progress and the American dream.

One topic the book addresses is Abraham Lincoln and his freeing of slaves in the United States. Lincoln is often presented as the great emancipator of the slaves, but his primary goal was to save the Union during the Civil War, regardless of how slaves were affected.

States also subjugated and destroyed the indigenous peoples. As a result, the Native American population was nearly decimated, their lives dramatically changed from one of independence to one of deep struggle.

FORCED REMOVAL

In 1607, English settlers began arriving in the New World. The colonists began settling land occupied by the indigenous people—Native Americans—and relying on them for labor. However, the Native Americans were susceptible

Andrew Jackson's Role in Acquiring Native-American Lands

Andrew Jackson played a major role in the removal of Native Americans from their lands. In the 1810s, Jackson led military forces against tribes, defeating them and gaining millions of acres of land in the South. During the 1820s, Jackson negotiated treaties in which Native Americans gave up lands in the East for land in the West. These treaties gave the United States acreage in several southern states.

Jackson became US president in 1829. In that role, he continued supporting the removal of Native Americans from their lands. In 1830, he backed the Indian Removal Act, which gave him power to negotiate removal treaties with Native Americans living east of the Mississippi River. As with previous treaties, Native Americans would give up their lands in the East for land in the West. The trip west was extremely hard, even for those who agreed. Many had to walk the entire journey. The government did not provide the food and supplies that had been promised, and many died on the way.

The Cherokee nation migrated in 1838 and 1839. This group of Native Americans was forced to move to what is now Oklahoma. During the long journey, the 15,000 Cherokees marching westward struggled with hunger, exhaustion, and illness—4,000 died during the journey. The horror of the event resulted in the Cherokee people calling it the Trail of Tears.

to illnesses brought by the Europeans and were not useful to the landowners. But this did not provide a reprieve from the European settlers who continued to encroach on the land of Native Americans and disrupt their centuries-old ways of life.

Two centuries later, as settlers moved south and west from the original colonies, they intruded on the Native Americans who lived in these areas. For almost 30 years, the US government worked to remove Native Americans from their lands. During that time, there were wars with different Native-American nations, including three with the Seminoles that resulted in thousands of deaths and cost the federal government tens of millions of dollars. By 1837, the government had removed 46,000 Native Americans from their lands and signed treaties that led to the removal of Native Americans totaling an almost equal number. These removals gave the United States 25 million acres (10,117,141 ha) of land.

CENTURIES OF SLAVERY

While Native Americans' ways of life were disrupted by European settlers, so too were the lives of thousands of Africans. In 1619, the first Africans

arrived in the Virginia Colony, what is now the
state of Virginia in the United States. They did not
come by choice. Because Native Americans were
susceptible to illnesses brought by the Europeans,
the number of available laborers in the 1600s
dwindled. Landowners began using another option:
African slaves.

Africans were captured, sold as slaves, and
shipped to the British colonies in North America
in the storage holds of ships. There was no legalized
slavery in Virginia at the time, so the Africans were
technically indentured servants. They were sold to
colonists and required to work until the cost of the
voyage to North America was paid off, even though
the Africans were not in America willingly.

Many poor white immigrants were also
indentured servants. They were not captured and
sold, but many were tricked into coming to the new
land. Wealthy plantation owners needed people to
work the fields, and African and European—black
and white—indentured servants toiled together and
withstood harsh treatment. Before long, the groups
began to be treated differently as racist attitudes
against the Africans prevailed over class bias against
poor whites. African servants received harsher

Slaves were crammed into ships for transport to new lands in which they suffered terribly as slaves.

punishments and were required to work more years to pay off their debts than their white counterparts.

Eventually, Virginia plantation owners decided to pursue slaves as their primary source of labor. Two centuries of slavery followed, during which

Africans endured forced capture, horrendous and often lethal travel conditions, hard labor, brutal treatment, and an utter lack of freedom, including for their children. They could be sold or rented out to another plantation. Generation after generation was born into forced servitude, even though the children were born in America and were therefore Americans. The difference was an issue of race—more specifically, skin color.

THE ONE-DROP RULE

There is no scientific basis for determining race. Because of this, whites in power who chose to classify people by race were forced to invent methods for deciding who was black—African or African American—and who was white. These methods have changed over time and can seem arbitrary. In 1705, a Virginia law defined a person as black if he or she was more than one-eighth African—meaning one or more great-grandparent was an African or African American. By 1785, the law was changed to less than one-fourth—one or more grandparent was an African or African American. In 1910 and 1911, several states adopted what became known as a one-drop rule. The Arkansas version of the law declared a person an African American if there was "any negro blood whatever."[3]

These distinctions are important in understanding the invention and the scope of racism in the United States. Like the conquest of new lands, slavery was initiated for economic reasons. It was also founded on—and flourished because of—racism. Africans and African Americans were enslaved, not whites. Interracial unions were taboo. Though the Declaration of Independence granted previously unheard of freedoms when it was signed and adopted in 1776, these were not extended to all individuals in the United States.

SEPARATE AND UNEQUAL

Decades after slavery was abolished in 1865, African Americans endured continued discrimination through segregation in the South where slavery had been prominent before the Civil War (1861–1865). This was

Laws and Rulings Against Minorities

Federal laws and rulings have affected the ability of different groups to become naturalized citizens. The Naturalization Act of 1790 limited naturalization to whites. In *Ozawa v. United States* (1922) and *United States v. Bhagat Singh Thind* (1923), the Supreme Court declared Japanese and Asian Indians ineligible for citizenship because they were not white. In addition, the Immigration Act of 1924 limited the number of immigrants who could enter the United States. Many nations had a limit of 100 per year, including Afghanistan, Bulgaria, China, Greece, India, New Zealand, and Turkey. Other nations had much higher quotas: Denmark, 2,789; Great Britain and Northern Ireland, 34,007 (total); Italy, 3,845; and Sweden, 9,561.

often done through Jim Crow laws, which the 1896 Supreme Court ruling in *Plessy v. Ferguson* supported by establishing the "separate but equal" policy.

Segregated facilities become the norm. For almost a century, laws required blacks to use public facilities separate from whites. This extended to drinking fountains, bathrooms, schools, seating on public transportation, and movie theaters. This practice lasted until the 1950s. African Americans suffered harsh treatment and lesser services than whites. Hate crime, murder, and lynching were prevalent.

CHALLENGES FACED BY OTHER GROUPS

Other groups have also faced racism in the United States. Each new wave of immigrants has suffered from discrimination, bias, degradation, and stereotyping. Though Irish and Eastern Europeans were widely discriminated against, Asian Americans and Latinos—who, like blacks, are referred to as people of color—suffered the indignities and injustices born of racism.

In California, Mexican Americans and Asian Americans faced harsh working conditions on the railroad and discriminatory laws in gold mines. The

JIM CROW,

An illustration of Jim Crow, a stereotypical racist depiction of an African-American man dancing in a field. The term Jim Crow represented the segregated facilities in the South and the laws that provided for them.

territory of California was the property of Mexico before it was overtaken by the United States in the Mexican-American War (1846–1848). After the war, armed squatters and new tax laws forced wealthy Mexican-American landowners off their property. Laws established to maintain land rights for Mexican Americans were largely ignored.

In 1852, California's state assembly recommended a resolution that would make it illegal for many Mexicans, Asians, and South Americans to mine. The resolution did not pass the California Senate, so it was not sent to the US Congress. But in 1882, the US Congress passed the Chinese Exclusion Act. It was the first law to exclude immigration based on one's nationality.

The World War II Years

Such racism and discrimination continued into the 1900s and was magnified during World War II (1939–1945). When the United States joined the fight against white supremacist policies of Nazi Germany, some Americans began questioning racist practices at home. Approximately 900,000 African Americans joined the service during World War II, but they fought in a segregated military. Recognizing the irony of fighting prejudice with a segregated service, African-American leaders pressed the US government to desegregate the armed forces. In a letter to the National Association for the Advancement of Colored People (NAACP), a 22-year-old soldier wrote,

> *I won't fight or die in vain. If I fight, suffer or die it will be for the freedom of every black man to live equally with other races. If the life of the Negro in the United States is right as it is lived today, then I would rather be dead.* [4]

African Americans were given the least skilled jobs and were initially prohibited from entering the US Air Force. Later in the war, the War Department changed its policy and allowed African Americans to join that branch of the US military. Many Americans not serving in the military contributed to the war effort at home. But defense industry jobs were reserved for whites. African Americans continued to fight for justice while African-American soldiers fought bravely in the war.

Other groups were also treated discriminatorily during the war. Perhaps the most striking injustice

The Tuskegee Airmen

From 1941 to 1946, a group of black pilots trained at the Tuskegee Army Air Field in Alabama, becoming the first African-American pilots in the US military. Nearly 1,000 pilots graduated and received Army Air Corps silver pilot wings. These black pilots overcame racism in the United States and abroad while bravely serving their country during World War II.

In 1948, President Harry S. Truman issued an executive order that the military must offer equal treatment and opportunity for all. This paved the way for the desegregation of the armed forces and, eventually, all federal institutions.

was the internment of Japanese-American citizens. In 1941, the Japanese bombed the US naval installation at Pearl Harbor, Hawaii. In response, the United States declared war on Japan and officially entered World War II. In addition, the federal government ordered Japanese Americans placed in camps, fearing they posed some sort of threat against the United States. From 1942 to 1945, more than 100,000 Japanese Americans were forced from their homes and placed in camps.

After the war ended, the tide of racial disparity began to change. Thousands of people worked at varying levels to end centuries of discrimination by the white majority. Social change began taking place in the mid-1950s on a small scale with the actions of individuals. In Alabama, the act of one woman fueled the civil rights movement and led to dramatic progress toward creating equality among the races in the United States.

The Civil Liberties Act

On August 10, 1988, the US Congress passed the Civil Liberties Act. Designed to apologize to Japanese Americans for their internment during World War II, the act recognized that an injustice had been done. The act states, "For these fundamental violations of the basic civil liberties and constitutional rights of these individuals of Japanese ancestry, the Congress apologizes on behalf of the Nation."[5] In 1993, each internment victim received $20,000 and a signed letter of apology from President Bill Clinton. Many have argued that African Americans should receive a similar apology and funds in reparation for years of enforced slavery.

*A Japanese-American boy to be interned waited for his parents
under the watchful eye of a military policeman in 1942.*

*Rosa Parks's refusal to move to the back of a bus
got her arrested and fueled the civil rights movement.*

A Decade of Change

In December 1955, a well-educated woman
named Rosa Parks rode a city bus in
Montgomery, Alabama, home from work. She had a
seat in the fifth row, the first of the rows reserved for
African-American passengers. The bus filled quickly

and soon the rows available to white passengers were fully occupied. As was the norm at the time, the white bus driver asked Parks, because she was an African American, to get up and let a white man have her seat. She refused and was arrested.

After paying a fine and bail, Parks and her husband met with the local branch of the NAACP, of which Parks was a member. Despite the potential threat to her life, Parks decided to let her arrest be used as a challenge to the degrading and firmly established bus segregation laws. Parks's case led to a successful boycott of Montgomery's public buses by the city's African Americans.

The Boycott

History shows that economics often plays a role in perpetuating racism. But when people band together, economics can work against racism as well. Civil rights leaders and community activists have successfully used economic tactics to win support for their goals.

In 1955, African Americans accounted for nearly three-fourths of the passengers on Montgomery's buses. After Parks was arrested and fined, a local pastor named Martin Luther King Jr. and the

NAACP asked Montgomery's citizens to stop riding the city's buses for one day. They hoped to gain a milder form of segregation, one in which they would be treated with respect and not be asked to move from the areas of the bus designated for blacks to make room for whites.

Nearly the entire African-American community did not ride the bus that first day. The success of the boycott prompted a hostile response from the bus company and the majority of whites in power. This

Brown v. Board of Education

The 1896 Supreme Court ruling in *Plessy v. Ferguson* that legalized separate but equal facilities was overturned by the landmark case *Brown v. Board of Education* in 1954. This case was a combination of five lawsuits brought by African-American parents seeking equal education for their children.

Sociologist Kenneth Clark testified in some of the five cases. He studied the effects of segregation and racism on African-American children by showing them a black doll and a white doll and asking which the children liked best. African-American children tended to identify the white doll with positive characteristics, such as being nicer or more fun to play with. Clark emphasized that the separate but unequal schools sent a clear message to African-American children that they were somehow undeserving of quality facilities. This negatively affected their self-esteem, which is why the children perceived the white dolls as being better than the black dolls.

The legal team argued that discrimination based on racial segregation "violates the 14th amendment to the U.S. Constitution, which guarantees all citizens equal protection of the laws."[1] The ruling effectively ended legalized segregation in schools and other public facilities. It paved the way for the civil rights movement and marked a turning point for democracy and justice in the United States.

encouraged the protesters to expand their demands. Rather than simply be treated more courteously, they asked for a complete desegregation of the city's transportation system.

Through immense communal organization—and at great personal inconvenience—Montgomery's African-American community found alternate transportation for one year. Seeing such large losses in profits as a result of the boycott, white business owners in the downtown area took the protesters' side and tried to help negotiate a truce with the bus company. But the bus company continued to argue for segregation, suggesting that desegregation would result in violence on the buses.

Months later, the case went to court. The judge ruled in favor of the boycotters in 1956. Montgomery's buses were desegregated.

The Little Rock Nine

The following year, in September 1957, desegregation continued in the South as nine African-American students in Little Rock, Arkansas, led the charge in integrating the city's all-white high school. The teenagers were enrolled in an all-white high school for the first time. On the first day of classes, eight of the nine teenagers walked to Central High School in the company of adults from the NAACP. The Arkansas National Guard met them at the door and kept them from entering. Governor Orval Faubus had directed the soldiers to prevent the students from entering.

The eight students were turned away, but the last student, Elizabeth Eckford, went to school on her own. When she got off the bus, an angry mob went toward her, shouting. A white woman and a reporter helped Eckford to safety before she was hurt by the white students.

In preventing school integration, Faubus acted against a federal law that had passed three years earlier. President Dwight D. Eisenhower ordered the governor to allow the students to attend classes. Faubus refused, so Eisenhower sent 1,000 paratroopers from the US Army to escort the teens to school.

The troops stayed for 60 days and were replaced by guards who stayed for the full school year, ensuring the safety of the nine black students as they entered and exited the school. But inside the school, the students endured taunts and cruelty from the majority of their white classmates. Still, all but

Seven of the nine students known as the Little Rock Nine were escorted to their high school by National Guard troops in October 1957.

one of the black students finished the school year at Central High. The following fall, Faubus closed the school to prevent further integration. This action was ruled unconstitutional. When Central High reopened in 1960, it was an integrated school.

Tumultuous Change

The Little Rock episode brought the nation's attention to the plight of African Americans under

Jim Crow laws. Across the country, blacks—and many whites—angry at decades of injustice, began to fight for change. Many also fought against change.

Throughout the 1950s and 1960s, King led nonviolent protests against racial segregation. College students initiated the integration of lunch counters, which was a popular form of dining at that time. Black and white activists worked together to integrate the country's buses and trains.

Many peaceful protests were met with violence by angry whites intent on keeping segregation in

"In a sense we have come to our nation's capital to cash a check. When the architects of our republic wrote the magnificent words of the Constitution and the Declaration of Independence, they were signing a promissory note to which every American was to fall heir. This note was a promise that all men, yes, black men as well as white men, would be guaranteed the unalienable rights of life, liberty, and the pursuit of happiness."[2]
—Martin Luther King, August 28, 1963

place. In Alabama, volunteers on a Freedom Ride, designed to integrate the country's transportation system, were attacked. Several needed hospitalization.

As the civil rights movement gained ground, tension and violence increased. It came to a head in Birmingham, Alabama. In May 1963, King organized a nonviolent protest with 700 schoolchildren. When the children began to march, they were rounded up and arrested. A second protest was scheduled for the next day. This time, snarling police dogs and a barrage of water from industrial fire hoses greeted the children. The violence of the police reaction stunned a watching nation and world.

"We declare our right on this earth . . . to be a human being, to be respected as a human being, to be given the rights of a human being in this society, on this earth, in this day, which we intend to bring into existence *by any means necessary.*"[3]

—*Malcolm X*

MALCOLM X

King was not the only African-American leader in the civil rights movement. Malcolm X was another strong African-American voice arguing for and encouraging change in the treatment of African Americans in the United States. Like King, Malcolm X was a strong speaker. His approach was different from King's. Malcolm X expressed the anger and frustration he and other African Americans felt rather than highlighting the hope for integration King did in speeches such as "I Have a Dream."

While King tended to advocate nonviolence, Malcolm X promoted violence if necessary. He advocated black power and the importance of his fellow African Americans to defend themselves. King spoke mostly in the South, focusing on integration. Malcolm X expressed his views in New York City.

Black Panther Party

The Black Panther Party was founded in Oakland, California, in 1966 by African Americans Huey Newton and Bobby Seale to protect African-American residents against the police, who often brutalized them. The group eventually grew to more than 2,000 members with chapters in major US cities, including Chicago. Over time, the group became more revolutionary, building on the teachings of Malcolm X and spreading a view that had become more radical. This included arming African Americans and releasing African-American prisoners from jail. Violence between group members and police erupted in the 1960s and 1970s. The group lost members and eventually changed its focus from violence to social service. The Black Panther Party ended in the 1980s.

He also spoke at prestigious universities such as Harvard and Oxford, highlighting African-American identity, independence, and integrity. He also helped change how African Americans were identified: the words *Negro* and *colored* were later replaced with *black* and *Afro-American*. This helped change how African Americans were viewed.

CIVIL RIGHTS ACT

Although their approaches and focuses were different, King and Malcolm X ultimately shared the similar experience of racism and discrimination and had the same goal: equal treatment of African Americans. The efforts of King, Malcolm X, and countless Americans who fought for the cause of equality were not without results.

In June 1963, a month after the violence in Birmingham, President John F. Kennedy demanded that the

US Congress pass a civil rights bill that would end legalized segregation. In an impassioned speech to the nation, Kennedy said,

> *The heart of the question is whether all Americans can be afforded equal rights and opportunities, whether we are going to treat our fellow Americans as we want to be treated.*[4]

In August 1963, King led the March on Washington for Jobs and Freedom. More than 250,000 people of all races attended in support of equal rights for all. King gave his now famous "I Have a Dream" speech at this march.

In November 1963, Kennedy was assassinated. His successor, Lyndon Baines Johnson, asked Congress to pass the bill to honor their fallen leader. It passed in the House but was stalled by a filibuster, a long speech designed to delay legislative action, in the Senate. Johnson continued to press for the passage of civil rights legislation, expanding on Kennedy's original bill. The Senate passed the Civil Rights Act of 1964 in June. Johnson signed the act into law on July 2, which prohibited discrimination based on race, color, ethnicity, and religion.

After continued violence, including the murder of three white civil rights workers registering

African Americans to vote, Johnson signed the Voting Rights Act into law in 1965. It protected African Americans' right to vote. He also signed the 1965 Immigration and Nationality Act into law that year. It abolished the immigration quotas established decades earlier.

There were huge losses in the fight for civil rights as well. Malcolm X was shot and killed in 1965. King suffered the same fate when he was assassinated in 1968. The fight for civil rights was challenging and violent, but blacks and other groups were gaining in equality. Still, racism was far from being eradicated.

"There is no negro problem . . . there is no Southern problem, there is no Northern problem. There is only an American problem."[5]

—President Lyndon B. Johnson, March 15, 1965

*Martin Luther King Jr., left, and Malcolm X
had different styles for achieving the same goal of equality.*

*White and black students studied together
at Clinton High School in Clinton, Tennessee, in 1964.*

EDUCATION FOR ALL

In the 1950s, progress had been made
toward racial equality. However, by the
beginning of the twenty-first century, public schools
in the United States still remained deeply divided
along racial and economic lines. A report issued

by the Civil Rights Project at Harvard University in August 2002 noted a lack of exposure of races to one another in US schools:

> The racial trend in the school districts studied is substantial and clear: virtually all school districts analyzed are showing lower levels of inter-racial exposure since 1986, suggesting a trend towards resegregation, and in some districts, these declines are sharp.[1]

Studies revealed steep differences in funding, test scores, course offerings, and graduation rates between schools serving primarily white children and those serving primarily children of color. Segregation had been proven unconstitutional, but education still was not equal.

School Funding

Public schools are funded in large part by money that comes from property taxes. As a result, schools in wealthier areas, where a majority of white families live, have access to

"We're really living a dichotomy now. It's a tale of two nations. The avenues to success are there for many people, but not there for many others. We're at the point when the questions regarding race and education are much more complicated, more a reflection of access—the kind of access some African Americans have and others do not."[2]
—*David J. Dent, author of* In Black America, *in response to a 2000 survey of the status of African-American families*

more money than schools in poorer areas, where a
majority of students of color attend school. In *Between
Barack and a Hard Place: Racism and White Denial in the Age of
Obama*, Tim Wise addressed race in the United States
in the twenty-first century:

> The average black student, for instance, attends a school
> with twice as many low-income students as the typical
> white youth, and schools that are mostly attended by black
> and Latino students are more than ten times as likely as
> mostly white schools to be schools with concentrated levels
> of student poverty.[3]

Linda Darling-Hammond of Stanford
University's School of Education addressed the issue
of opportunity for students of color as well:

> Recent analyses of data prepared for school finance cases
> in Alabama, New Jersey, New York, Louisiana, and
> Texas have found that on every tangible measure—from
> qualified teachers to curriculum offerings—schools serving
> greater numbers of students of color had significantly fewer
> resources than schools serving mostly white students.[4]

The substantial monetary gap between schools
serving mostly white students and those serving
mostly students of color results in a disparity of
resources. This includes books, paper, desks,

facilities, and teachers who are qualified and certified—the essentials every student needs.

The Equal Opportunity Question

Even before children attend school, they learn from parents, other family members, and their community. Cultural and economic diversity play a role in what a child learns before attending school. Opportunity begins with education. The racial and economic imbalance in US education has a profound impact on the future success of students. High levels of poverty in a school community compound stressors on students. These can include family unemployment, community violence, and inadequate health care, nutrition, and early education. All of these play a role in establishing equal educational opportunities for all.

It is too simplistic to conclude that African-American, Latino, or Asian-American children are less prepared

Teach for America

Teach for America is a nonprofit organization striving to limit the educational differences afforded children of color by providing well-trained teachers to low-income schools in almost 40 areas. By recruiting and training recent college graduates to teach in these schools, the organization aims "to build the movement to eliminate educational inequity by enlisting our nation's most promising future leaders in the effort."[5]

for school due to economic disparity or language differences because there are numerous examples to the contrary. Even though more white children come from wealthy families where education is valued, there are scores of poor white children who are not prepared for school success. But an overwhelming number of children of color live in poverty and attend underfunded schools.

Affirmative Action

Higher education also faces challenges

Fifty Years after *Brown*

Brown v. Board of Education put an end to separate but equal, but research has shown this has not been the case. In 2004, Harvard University's Gary Orfield and Chungmei Lee published Brown *at 50: King's Dream or the* Plessy *Nightmare.* The report addresses US education in the decades following the *Brown* ruling. The report had several key findings:

- *There has been a substantial slippage toward segregation in most of the states that were highly desegregated in 1991. . . .*
- *Asians are the most integrated and most successful group of students. . . .*
- *Most white students have little contact with minority students except in the South and Southwest.*
- *The vast majority of intensely segregated minority schools face conditions of concentrated poverty, which are powerfully related to unequal educational opportunity. . . .*
- *Latinos confront very serious levels of segregation by race and poverty. . . .*
- *In some states with very low black populations, school segregation is soaring as desegregation efforts are abandoned.*[6]

Orfield noted of the findings, "Martin Luther King's dream is being celebrated in theory and dishonored in practice with the decisions and methods that [are] re-segregating our schools."[7]

regarding race. US colleges and universities
have struggled with ways to remedy the
underrepresentation of African Americans, Latinos,
and Native Americans in their programs since the
1960s. Perhaps the most widely debated program
to resolve this issue is affirmative action. This term
refers to a set of practices intended to help schools
and other institutions achieve greater diversity. The
concept has generated much debate and numerous
challenges.

Initially intended to offset the majority of
whites admitted to institutions of higher learning,
affirmative action is often misunderstood as a set
of quotas and excessive scholarships. Some
people claim affirmative action promotes reverse
discrimination, placing whites at a disadvantage
because institutions fulfill quotas rather than
acknowledge qualifications.

Roger Clegg is the president of the Center for
Equal Opportunity. The organization "supports
colorblind public policies and seeks to block the
expansion of racial preferences and to prevent their
use in employment, education, and voting."[8] Clegg
noted of affirmative action,

In October 1995, demonstrators protested the University of California's decision to scrap affirmative action policies at the institution.

Quotas do not end discrimination. They are discrimination. The law makes clear that race, ethnicity and sex are not to be part of who gets a government contract or who gets into a university or where someone goes to school.[9]

But contrary to popular belief, schools are not mandated to admit minority students, qualified or not. Instead, affirmative action allows university officials to take race into account—along with many other factors—when considering applicants.

The many misunderstandings about affirmative action prompted sociologist Fred L. Pincus to write a book on the topic: *Reverse Discrimination: Dismantling the Myth*. In relation to scholarship monies, Pincus noted, "According to the American Council on Education, less than 3% of minority students received scholarships specially designed for minorities. This accounted for 2% of all aid to college students."[10]

Still, the debate over affirmative action continues. In some states, voters have been given the opportunity to decide on its continued existence. Perhaps most notable is California's Proposition 209. In 1996, the proposition to modify California's constitution by removing affirmative action programs was approved. The law has since been challenged in court, but rulings have kept it in place. California is not alone in addressing affirmative action. Voters in Washington passed a similar ban in 1998, followed by

Bakke v. University of California

In 1978, a white student named Alan Bakke sued the University of California at Davis Medical School for discrimination. Bakke argued that the school had admitted students less qualified than he was by setting aside 16 percent of seats for minority applicants. The case went to the US Supreme Court, which ruled in favor of the student, and Bakke was admitted.

Michigan in 2006 and Nebraska in
2008. Clegg noted, "The laws that
Congress wrote are clear—everyone is
protected from racial discrimination.
Not just blacks, but whites. Not just
Latinos, but whites."[11]

Dennis Parker, director of the
American Civil Liberties Union's
Racial Justice Project, disagrees.
Parker has discussed the racial
disparity that continues in the United
States. In 2009, he said,

March on Washington

On April 1, 2003, the
Coalition to Defend Affirmative Action marched
on Washington DC to
empower affirmative
action and defend the
rights put in place by
*Brown v. Board of Edu-
cation.* Approximately
200,000 people attended
in support of the cause.

We like to believe there is an equal playing field. In fact, there
isn't. In this country, whites are still advantaged in many
ways. You can say we shouldn't take race into consideration,
but that just continues the advantage. . . . Clearly there have
been changes. We have a black president. But if I were to go
into any office on Wall Street, I think it would be hard to
deny that white people aren't getting jobs. You wouldn't see
a lot of black people and women.[12]

While people continue to debate the issue of
affirmative action, examples remain that support
the argument that racial disparity exists, not only in
education, but in other areas.

In October 1995, University of California—Los Angeles students protested their school's decision to no longer have affirmative action policies.

Some of the thousands of displaced residents took cover from Hurricane Katrina at the Superdome in New Orleans, Louisiana, in August 2005.

A CASE STUDY
IN DISPARITY

The issue of race and resources became the center of attention during the hurricane season of 2005. In August of that year, Hurricane Katrina struck the Gulf Coast of the United States with devastating effect. Louisiana was hardest hit with the majority of the damage concentrated in the city of New Orleans. The Lower Ninth Ward, a historically African-American community, suffered extensive damage.

On television and via the Internet, viewers in the United States and abroad watched the disaster unfold. The hurricane was responsible for more than 1,800 deaths and $80 million in property damages. Images of men and women from the Lower Ninth Ward, mostly black and living in poverty, were seen around the world as they struggled to survive.

In 2005, approximately two-thirds of the citizens of New Orleans were African American. The city also had one of the highest rates of child poverty in the nation at 38 percent in 2000. Approximately 20 percent of the families had no access to a car. Without means of

Lilly Ledbetter Fair Pay Act

Despite achievements in academia, business, government, and the arts and sciences, people of color still faced inequalities at the beginning of the twenty-first century. For example, minorities— and women—held fewer supervisory positions and were paid less than white male counterparts.

In January 2009, President Barack Obama signed the Lilly Ledbetter Fair Pay Act into law. It was designed to override a 2007 Supreme Court decision on discriminatory pay in any case, but specifically against women. Obama said of the law, "I intend to send a clear message: That making our economy work means making sure it works for everyone. That there are no second class citizens in our workplaces."[1]

transportation, it was impossible to leave the city. Although many residents of all races were able to flee before the storm made landfall, those without cars or other transportation were unable to leave the city as the hurricane approached. A levee broke and water flooded the streets, businesses, and homes. Thousands of residents were stranded.

RESPONDING TO THE STORM

The water rushing through the streets and buildings of New Orleans was filled with pollution. Stranded people rode hastily made rafts and stood on rooftops. Dead bodies floated in the water. Survivors made their way or were taken to the city's sports arena where violence broke out in response to cramped conditions and limited resources.

The federal emergency response to the disaster was widely decried as insufficient and slow, and President George W. Bush was widely criticized for his administration's handling of the crisis. Evacuation efforts lagged. The president, on vacation, gave brief speeches about the disaster before arriving in the Gulf Coast four days after the storm hit. He visited Alabama, which had suffered damage to a considerably lesser degree.

On September 12, 2005, two weeks after Katrina struck, Bush responded to criticisms that the recovery effort was discriminatory. The president said, "The storm didn't discriminate and neither will the recovery effort."[2]

A Growing Gap

Three days later, on September 15, Bush acknowledged the situation in New Orleans in an address to the nation. This time, he addressed the complex economic and racial aspects of the tragedy. Referencing the poverty of the region many

Jobless Rates

The Center for American Progress reports that in 2008, "minorities were at least more than 40 percent more likely than whites to experience unemployment at the end of 2008."[3] Two recent studies highlight possible reasons for the disparity.

In 2002, Devah Pager published *The Mark of a Criminal Record*, which describes and reports her study of race and discrimination in the job market. Pager submitted fictitious résumés in response to job openings in Milwaukee, Wisconsin. Pager found that white men with a criminal record were more likely to get a response from potential employers than African Americans without a record.

Marianne Bertrand and Sendhil Mullainathan also studied race and discrimination in the job market using fictitious résumés. The duo published the findings of their experiment in *Are Emily and Greg more Employable than Lakisha and Jamal? A Field Experiment On Labor Market Discrimination*. In their study, Bertrand and Mullainathan sent out fake résumés to possible employers in Boston, Massachusetts, and Chicago, Illinois, in response to newspaper ads. The study found that résumés with African-American sounding names were much less likely to generate interest, even when credentials were identical.

saw in footage from the storm-damaged area,
he said, "Poverty has roots in a history of racial
discrimination, which cut off generations from the
opportunity of America. We have a duty to confront
this poverty with bold action."[4]

But bold action was not in evidence during
the long months of recovery. Reports that the
Federal Emergency Management Agency (FEMA)
had mismanaged the disaster were widespread. In
December 2005, four months after the storm,
community activists and victims of Katrina testified
about their experiences in New Orleans to a
congressional committee. Victims stated that racism
had contributed to the government's slow response
time. Five years after the disaster, large sections
of New Orleans, particularly African-American
communities such as the Lower Ninth Ward, were
still in a state of disrepair.

Katrina and its aftermath pointed to the often
silent but persistent economic difference between
African Americans and whites in the United States.
But New Orleans is also home to many middle-class
Americans of both races. The disaster revealed the
dramatic gap between Americans of all colors with
regard to wealth.

As images of the Lower Ninth Ward were televised around the world, viewers saw firsthand the deep poverty of that African-American neighborhood. Americans were confronted with the often ignored problems of poverty and racism. The pictures of suffering reinforced the fact that, proportionately, African Americans are more likely to live in poverty than white Americans. This holds true across the nation and for other groups. African-American and Latino families have considerably less wealth than white families. G. William Domhoff, a sociology professor at the University of California at Santa Cruz, has studied income and wealth in the United States. He noted a disparity in wealth based on race, writing, "In 2007, the average white household had 15 times as much total wealth as the average African-American or Latino household."[5]

Income versus Wealth

While income and wealth both concern money, the two are different. Income is what a person earns from a job. Wealth is what a person has in savings and resources, such as real estate.

African-American veterans of World War II faced challenges in obtaining benefits granted to their white counterparts. This is often referred to as the "affirmative action" for whites because the government subsidized the growth of suburbia with the GI Bill and the Veterans Administration loans to buy homes. These slights are in large part responsible for the wealth gaps between African Americans and whites seen in the late nineteenth and early twentieth centuries.

Equal Employment Opportunities Act

In 1972, President Richard M. Nixon signed the Equal Employment Opportunities Act into law. The act is designed to prevent employment discrimination for any reason, including race.

The discrimination and racism experienced by people of color in the United States has been evident in statistical data on education and employment. It has been highlighted in news stories about Hurricane Katrina. But the differential treatment of people of color has been evident in other ways—the most harmful of which have been hate crimes, particularly those resulting in abuse and murder.

New Orleans residents walked through floodwaters following Hurricane Katrina in August 2005.

Stella and James Byrd Sr. arranged flowers at the grave of their son James Byrd Jr., who was the victim of a horrendous hate crime.

HATE CRIMES

On a Sunday morning in June 1998, neighbors outside of Jasper, Texas, discovered the body of a man who had been dragged to death behind a pickup truck. The body was mutilated. The victim was 49-year-old James Byrd Jr.

Byrd, an African American, did not own a car and received disability payments from the government. He often walked or accepted rides from neighbors in Jasper where he lived with his family. On the night he was killed, Byrd reportedly was offered a ride from three men in a truck. The men did not take Byrd home. Instead, they took him to the woods, beat him, chained him to a truck, and dragged him to his death.

Three white men where charged, tried, and convicted of Byrd's brutal killing. Two of the men had racist tattoos and supported the white supremacist group Ku Klux Klan (KKK). The crime was concluded to be racially motivated. The two KKK supporters were sentenced to death. The third man, who was deemed by a jury to not be a future menace to society, was sentenced to life in prison.

The murder appalled citizens of Jasper and beyond. The NAACP and other civil rights groups condemned the killing. Speaking out against the crime, President Bill Clinton urged the residents of the town to "join across racial lines to demonstrate that an act of evil like this is not what this country is all about."[1]

A History of Abuse

Byrd's murder was shocking and tragic. It also served as a reminder of the nation's past. In August 1955, one year after the monumental case *Brown v. Board of Education* ended legalized segregation, a similar story gripped the nation. Emmett Till, a black teenager from Chicago, was visiting relatives in the Mississippi Delta during his summer vacation. The visit ended in tragedy when Till was taken from his relative's home, beaten, and killed. Two white men were accused of killing the teen. Though widely acknowledged as the killers, the men were acquitted in court in a ruling that outraged many Americans.

The men claimed Till had flirted with one of their wives. Till's story tapped into a long history of racist stereotyping and fear of black men. In an analysis of the murder in his book *A Death in the Delta: The Story of Emmett Till*, author Stephen J. Whitfield explained the racist climate in the South at the time: "The preservation of white patriarchy seemed to require the suppression of even the most insignificant challenges to its authority."[2]

Though Till was only one of many African Americans viciously killed long after the end of slavery and before the start of integration, his

Emmett Till

murder shocked the nation. The teen's tragic death
fueled the civil rights movement.

The years between the two crimes produced
multiple changes in both legislation and in cultural
attitudes. Byrd's murder was shocking for reasons

different from Till's murder. Byrd's death came at a time when federal institutions had been legally integrated for more than half a century. Prior to Byrd's murder, many Americans may have believed such racist crimes to be a thing of the past.

KEEPING HATE CRIMES STATISTICS

Acts of violence perpetrated against a victim because of race are called hate crimes. In 1990, the US Congress passed the Hate Crime Statistics Act, which President George H. W. Bush signed into law. The law marked the beginning of data collection on national hate crimes. The FBI was given the responsibility of collecting statistics. Since 1992, the FBI has gathered and published hate crime statistics annually. According to CNN, Attorney General Eric Holder told the Senate Judiciary Committee in June 2009:

> More than 77,000 hate-crime incidents had been reported by the FBI between 1998 and 2007, or "nearly one hate crime for every hour of every day over the span of a decade."[3]

Racism is one of the major causes of hate crimes, but other forms of discrimination also motivate hate crimes. The FBI hate crime data includes "crimes that manifest evidence of prejudice based on race, religion, sexual orientation, and ethnicity."[4] In 1994, under the Violent Crime Control and Law Enforcement Act, physical and mental disabilities were added as factors that could be a basis for hate crimes. The FBI recorded 9,692 hate crimes in the United States in 2008. Of those, 51 percent were racially motivated.

PERPETRATORS OF HATE CRIMES

People of all races perpetrate hate crimes. Often, there is a more active ringleader and others who

Matthew Shepard

In 2009, the FBI reported that hate crimes because of sexual orientation increased in 2008. This could be due, in part, to an increased number of agencies reporting the crimes or an increase in victims speaking out.

In October 1998, Matthew Shepard, 21, was kidnapped, tortured, and killed by two men in Wyoming because he was gay. The incident brought national attention to this issue of hate crimes against homosexuals.

Shepard's parents, Dennis and Judy Shepard, started a foundation in memory of their son. The foundation supports diversity programs in education that promote tolerance, compassion, understanding, respect, and acceptance. Programs include fighting for anti-hate crime legislation, providing resources and an outlet for gay youth to share their stories and make their voices heard, and joining other groups nationwide and around the world to fight hate and promote understanding.

In October 2009, the US Senate voted to expand the definition of a hate crime to include crimes against a person due to bias regarding sexual orientation or gender identity. The bill was named the Matthew Shepard and James Byrd Jr. Hate Crimes Prevention Act.

go along with the act. People regularly consider personal prejudice to be racism, but studies of group gang-up hate crimes reveal that individual bigotry is not the only factor at play. Social conformity and peer pressure are also factors. Participants might be trying to prove their masculinity to their peers or trying to fit in with a group.

White Americans commit the majority— approximately two-thirds—of the hate crimes in the United States each year. In 1993, Northeastern University professors Jack Levin and Jack McDevitt studied hate crimes to gain an understanding of the perpetrators. Their research found the majority of hate crimes to be committed by white men in their teens or early twenties.

Hate Crimes in 2008

According to the FBI, the more than 9,500 victims of hate crimes in the United States during 2008 were targeted as follows:

- Race: 4,943
- Religion: 1,732
- Sexual orientation: 1,706
- Ethnicity/national origin: 1,226
- Disability: 85

The professors divided offenders into three categories. The researchers estimate that more than half of hate crimes in the United States are impromptu or impulsive acts. Members of the next largest group of young white offenders tend to see themselves as defending their territory or way of life. The third and smallest group of offenders includes members of hate groups such as the KKK and Aryan Nation. These groups also tend to be the most dangerous. Hate groups such as these had waned over the past century, but in recent years, they have begun to use the Internet to recruit young Americans.

VICTIMS OF HATE CRIMES

African Americans are at the greatest risk for hate crimes. People from various ethnic backgrounds are also at risk for hate crimes. From the earliest days of the nation, new immigrants to the United States have been targets for prejudice, including being blamed for the social and economic problems in the country. For example, in 1982, Vincent Chin was beaten to death because he was Asian. At the time, the US auto industry was suffering with the rise in popularity of Japanese autos among Americans. As a result, many autoworkers in Detroit, Michigan, the nation's automotive center, were laid off.

Ronald Ebens got into a fight with Chin at a bar, blaming the Asian man for what was happening with the US auto industry. Japanese were blamed for US plant closings and layoffs. Chin was a Chinese American, but many Americans often do not discern between the various Asian groups. Ebens's stepson, Michael Nitz, had recently lost his job at an auto plant. Ebens and Nitz followed Chin from the bar and beat him to death with a baseball bat.

In recent years, anti-immigrant sentiment against Americans of Mexican, Central American, and South American descent has risen. Latinos have increasingly become victims of hate crimes since reporting began.

Arab Americans have also suffered from hate crimes, particularly since the attacks on the World Trade Center in September 2001. These crimes have included beatings and murders. Although the victims of hate crimes had nothing to do with the violence of 9/11, they are targeted because of their ethnic and racial background, just as Chin was blamed for the problems faced by the auto industry.

But placing blame on people based on race does not always occur on a singular level among one or two individuals. Sometimes, it happens on a broader level among members of an institution.

The KKK has a long history of committing hate crimes in the United States.

*For many young minority members,
a stay in prison has become a rite of passage.*

RACE AND THE LAW

During the 1960s and 1970s, crime in the United States rose dramatically. Politicians responded with stronger crime prevention agendas and tougher sentencing laws. Since that time, the number of Americans incarcerated has increased by more than 500 percent.

In 2010, more than 2 million Americans were incarcerated. Approximately 60 percent of those imprisoned were racial or ethnic minorities. Research shows an alarming racial disparity across the criminal justice system, including the number of arrests, type of sentencing, and length of jail time. Although African Americans make up 13 percent of the US population, they comprise 40 percent of the prison population.

In a 2007 report by the Sentencing Project, a national organization dedicated to fair and effective criminal justice, Marc Mauer and Ryan S. King found the rate of imprisonment for black males had increased steadily since the 1970s. Since 1990, the rate of incarceration for Latinos had increased 43 percent. The report found that Hispanic Americans were more than twice as likely and black Americans were more than five times as likely to be imprisoned than white Americans.

Roots of Inequity

Opinions differ about why there are so many more blacks and, more recently, Latinos, in

US prisons. Some researchers point to institutional racism within the criminal justice system. Others affirm the rates reflect the amount of crimes committed.

Prior to 1980, the majority of prisoners were white, not black. This is the one area where disparity between the races has increased since the 1960s. Many analysts blame the government's war on drugs of the 1980s, coupled with its war on crime in the 1990s, for this change. The economy has also played a role. There was an economic shift from industry to service that left inner cities, which is where many blacks live, without sources of income or services. This concentrated poverty.

Manning Marable is a professor of history and political science and the director of the Institute for Research in African-American Studies at Columbia University. He has expressed an urgent need to address racial disparity in the prison system. Marable has cited examples

Marable on Crime Prevention

In his discussion of crime and race in the United States, Manning Marable addressed crime prevention during the sixties and seventies. Marable wrote, "Behind much of anti-crime rhetoric was a not-too-subtle racial dimension, the projection of crude stereotypes about the link between criminality and black people. Rarely did these politicians observe that minority and poor people, not the white middle class, were statistically much more likely to experience violent crimes of all kinds."[1]

of racial inequity across the criminal justice system—
from arrests to sentencing to jail time—regardless of
offenses. This kind of inequity is most apparent in
the statistics about drug offenses. Marable pointed
to deep-seated stereotypes and characterizations
of African Americans as one of the causes of this
inequity. He noted,

> *The pattern of racial bias in these statistics is confirmed by*
> *the research of the US Commission on Civil Rights, which*
> *found that while African Americans today constitute only*
> *14% of all drug users nationally, they are 35% of all drug*
> *arrests, 55% of all drug convictions, and 75% of all prison*
> *admissions for drug offenses.* [2]

Sociologists Bruce Western and Becky Pettit
have studied the role of race in prison statistics.
In addition to relating the wars on crime and
drugs to prison statistics, the researchers have also
highlighted the importance of education. For many
poor African-American young men, prison is a
benchmark event, much like joining the military
or entering college is a benchmark for many young
men. The most influential factor on whether or
not a young man experiences the benchmark event
of going to prison is whether or not he graduates

from high school. The researchers addressed the issue, including the long-term effects of this benchmark, in their 2002 article, "Beyond Crime and Punishment: Prisons and Inequality":

> Changes in government policy on crime and punishment have put many poor minority men behind bars, more than their arrest rates would indicate. The growth of the penal system has also obscured the extent of economic inequality and sowed the seeds for greater inequality in the future. . . . It is clear that going to prison is now extremely common for young black men and pervasive among young black men who have dropped out of school. Imprisonment adds to the baggage carried by poorly educated and minority men, making it harder for them to catch up economically and further widening the economic gap between these men and the rest of society.[3]

RACIAL PROFILING

Law enforcement has affected people of color in other ways. Negative stereotypes have led to racial profiling, which is a term that refers to law enforcement officers targeting people of color. Comedians and some African Americans address racial profiling when they refer to being pulled over for "driving while black."[4]

The July 2009 arrest of Henry Louis Gates Jr., a celebrated Harvard professor of African-American studies, brought national attention and public debate to the complicated issue of racial profiling. Gates, an African American, was arrested when police responded to a call about a suspected burglary in his home. Gates's attorney claims the professor was arrested for breaking into his own home, but the police maintain the professor exhibited disorderly conduct when approached by the white officers who responded to the call and entered his home.

Some reports accused the white officers of racial

Amnesty International Reports on Racial Profiling

With almost 3 million supporters, Amnesty International is an international nonprofit organization that fights for human rights worldwide. The organization operates "independent of any government, political ideology, economic interest or religion."[5] It has offices worldwide, in more than 150 locations, including the United States.

In 2004, the Domestic Human Rights Program of Amnesty International USA issued a report on racial profiling. Based on one year of research and six public hearings, the report determined that racial profiling has impacted nearly 32 million Americans and undermines national security. According to the report, racial profiling affects men and women of all ages and socioeconomic backgrounds. Racial profiling also "directly affects Native Americans, Asian Americans, Hispanic Americans, African Americans, Arab Americans, Persian Americans, American Muslims, many immigrants and visitors, and, under certain circumstances, white Americans."[6] Racial profiling was reported to occur in all areas of life, while walking, driving, shopping, traveling to and from places of worship, at the airport, and even in private homes.

profiling; others faulted Gates for his response to the police. The diverse public opinion about this story revealed the complicated nature of this issue.

YOUTH IN PRISON

One of the most noteworthy trends in the US prison system is the increasing number of adolescents and young adults of color in the system. Marion Wright Edelman is the founder and president of the Children's Defense Fund and has been a leader of equal rights for children for decades. In her Child Watch column, Edelman wrote about youth in prison:

> *Nationally, one in three Black boys and one in six Latino boys born in 2001 are at risk of going to prison during their lifetimes. Although boys are more than five times as likely to be incarcerated as girls, the number of girls in the juvenile justice system is significant and growing.*[7]

Edelman refers to a complex set of factors that set children on a path that too often ends in the juvenile justice system. Factors include high rates of child poverty, incidence of parental incarceration, and lack of early childhood education and adequate health care. Edelman wrote, "America's cradle to

prison pipeline is putting thousands of young people
on a trajectory that leads to marginalized lives,
imprisonment, and often premature death."[8]

SOLUTIONS

Solutions to the racial disparity in the US prison
system tend to focus on the youngest prisoners.
Edelman and other youth advocates support early
intervention. This includes prevention over
punishment as well as treatment and
education over increasingly harsh
sentences and longer jail time.

Missouri's juvenile justice system
offers a model of effective detention
that integrates rehabilitation,
therapy, and education to help each
juvenile offender become more
productive and crime free. With only
8 percent of offenders returning to
detention and 8 percent going to
prison, Missouri's program provides
an important example of a successful
juvenile justice model for the nation.

The work of Reverend Greg
Boyle, a Jesuit priest in Los Angeles,

**A Successful Model
for Juvenile Detention**

The Models for Change
initiative—in Illinois,
Louisiana, Pennsylvania, Washington, and
12 partner states—promotes fairness, safety, and
responsibility in the juvenile justice system. One
approach of this successful program is to take into
account the developmental differences between
youth and adults when
detaining juveniles.

provides a successful model outside prison walls.
Boyle began his acclaimed work with former gang
members in East Los Angeles during the 1980s. His
work is based on the belief that a sense of community
and economic opportunity break the cycle of crime.
Boyle acts as a mentor to young men and women in
the neighborhood, including answering numerous
letters written to him from youth in prison.

In 1992, as a response to the Los Angeles riots,
Boyle started Homeboy Industries. The business
provides training, jobs, and opportunities for
former rival gang members to work side by side. The
core of this program is respect for each individual,
which includes acceptance. The organization's slogan
is Jobs not Jails. Homeboy Industries provides three
vital components for future success: community,
opportunity, and hope.

These factors were a focus of the first African-
American Democratic presidential candidate. In
2008, Barack Obama promoted change as part of his
campaign for president. That race and the election
were benchmarks in the history of the United States.

*As a children's advocate, Marion Wright Edelman
has expressed concern about youth in prison.*

Barack Obama's speech at the Democratic National Convention brought national attention to the then senator.

A Landmark Election

The 2004 Democratic National Convention brought a voice of hope to many Americans. The nation heard a new voice in US politics. The junior senator from Illinois, Barack Obama, gave a rousing speech. "There's not a liberal

America and a conservative America," Obama said. "There is the United States of America. There's not a black America and white America and Latino America and Asian America—there's the United States of America."[1]

When Obama spoke of unity, he was talking not only about his hope for the nation, but about his own experience. Obama's family is a mirror of 2.4 percent of the US population—approximately 6.8 million Americans, according to the 2000 census, who identify themselves as being of more than one race. Obama's mother and grandparents were white Americans, and his father was a black African from Kenya. The president still has many relatives in Kenya, and his half-sister, Maya Soetoro-Ng, is half Indonesian and married to a Canadian man of Chinese ancestry. Obama's wife, Michelle, is African American; her family includes descendents of slaves.

Gender and the 2008 Presidential Race

Hillary Clinton ran against Obama in the 2008 race for the Democratic nomination for president. Academic studies to determine the incidence of sexism during the campaign showed that Clinton received less press coverage than Obama—even when she was winning—and was more likely to be referred to by her first name, which could be interpreted as demonstrating less respect.

A VICTORY AND NEW STRIFE

Four years later, Obama actively pursued a loftier political role: US president. On August 28, 2008, the senator officially accepted his party's nomination for the presidential candidate. He became the first African-American presidential nominee of a major political party. Not all Americans were pleased by this. In response to increased threats against his life, Obama received Secret Service protection immediately after winning the primary. This was sooner than any other candidate in history. This was not the only evidence that some Americans feared the prospect of an African-American man as their president. As the long campaign drew on, and the Democratic ticket rose in the polls, the issue of race was used in increasingly inflammatory ways.

The Republican vice presidential nominee, Sarah Palin, began suggesting at campaign rallies that Obama associated with terrorists. Her comments incited voters to shout racist epithets and, at one point, to attack members of the press.

Record Turnout

The US Census Bureau reported that 131 million people turned out to vote in the 2008 presidential election. This was a 5 percent increase in voter turnout from the previous election in 2004. Data from a survey in which respondents self-identified showed a record turnout for African-American, Hispanic, and young voters, aged 18 to 24.

Columnist Mary Mitchell addressed the issue in the *Chicago Sun-Times*:

> As preposterous as her accusation was, it played to the fears of white voters who believe that Obama is too different from them to win the White House, but don't want to admit that they are prejudiced against him because he is black.[2]

In November 2008, Obama was elected the forty-fourth president of the United States. Two months later, in January 2009, a diverse group of more than 1 million Americans traveled to Washington DC to attend the inauguration of Obama, the first African-American president.

THE POLITICS OF RACE

During his campaign for the Democratic nomination, and then for the presidency, Obama did not emphasize his race. His chief campaign strategist, David Axelrod, stated the day after Obama won the presidential election, "He came to this not primarily as the black candidate, but as a candidate for president who happened to be black."[3]

This was a difficult but ultimately successful strategy. Journalist Gwen Ifill has covered US politics since the 1970s. She wrote of Obama's choice not to emphasize his race, explaining, "It was a fairly perilous tightrope that Obama walked, and one that had never been managed at this level before."[4] She added that Obama had to reach out to voters who might doubt him because of his race, while not alienating other voters. Ifill continued, "He did this in part by crafting his persona and his speeches to appeal to all listeners."[5] For example, Obama repeatedly used the theme and language of his 2004 speech by referring to a multiracial United States that included

Identity and the Obama Candidacy

Because Obama's family is so diverse, one might wonder why he is celebrated as the first African-American president. Race is not a scientific category, it is a social one. The United States has long defined biracial individuals according to the part of their background that descends from the least dominant racial minority. For example, a child with a white parent and an African-American parent would widely be considered African American.

Obama was raised by his mother and grandparents and met his father only once. Despite this, the president identifies with being African American. In his memoir, *Dreams from My Father*, Obama wrote about how he began to recognize himself as an African-American man in the United States, based largely on how he was treated by others. Like many children of mixed families, he realized that he was subtly treated differently than his mother and maternal grandparents. Also, as a young man who knew little of his father, he sought to understand and identify with his absent father's African heritage.

Obama's diverse personal history and professional achievements contribute to his empathy for all races and insistence that Americans work together for the common good. This is not an easy mission in a nation long divided by racial categories.

whites, African Americans, Asian Americans,
Latinos, Native Americans, and Arab Americans.

OBAMA SPEAKS OUT

In spring 2008, excerpts from sermons by
Reverend Jeremiah Wright were released on Internet
news and video sites. Many white voters were shocked
to hear the African-American preacher's angry
words against the United States. But voters familiar
with the style and rhetoric of African-American
churches defended Wright, explaining that his anger
was directed at the nation's treatment of African
Americans and other minorities. One member
of Wright's congregation said of the reverend's
approach, "I wouldn't call it radical. I call it being
black in America."[6]

Until this time, Obama had largely avoided
addressing his identity as an African American.
But his family's relationship with the pastor was
long—Wright had married the Obamas and baptized
their two daughters. His sermons posed the biggest
challenge to Obama of a difficult campaign thus far.

Initially, the candidate tried to distance himself
from the controversy. Then, on March 18, 2009,
the president spoke out, making his first speech

"Of course, the answer to the slavery question was already embedded within our Constitution—a Constitution that had at its very core the ideal of equal citizenship under the law; a Constitution that promised its people liberty and justice and a union that could be and should be perfected over time."[8]

—Barack Obama,
March 18, 2008

about race. He denounced his pastor's angry words, but Obama's speech also addressed issues that have long troubled the United States but were rarely discussed openly by politicians. He spoke of African Americans' anger at the legacy of slavery and white uncertainty about affirmative action. Directly speaking to his own relationship with race, Obama said,

Contrary to the claims of some of my critics, black and white, I have never been so naïve as to believe that we can get beyond our racial divisions in a single election cycle, or with a single candidacy. . . . I have asserted a firm conviction—a conviction rooted in my faith in God and my faith in the American people—that, working together, we can move beyond some of our old racial wounds, and that in fact we have no choice if we are to continue on the path of a more perfect union.[7]

Obama's swearing in on January 20, 2009, was a historic event for the United States that brought great hope to many Americans.

A man at Obama's inauguration shared the sentiments of many, but not all,
Americans as issues regarding race continue in the United States.

An Ongoing Issue

s the first African-American president,
Obama became a symbol of hope—in
the United States and around the world—for a
better future where differences do not divide but
unite. In the early days of his presidency, many

spoke enthusiastically of a post-racial America. But the evidence is clear that race remains a factor in the distribution of resources.

Not long after Obama took office, the National Urban League released its *2009 State of Black America* report. The findings showed that racial inequities continued in employment, housing, health care, education, criminal justice, and other areas. Journalist Leonard Pitts Jr. explored these findings and attempted to understand why so many people proclaimed a new post-racial nation when such evidence for racial inequity persists:

> *Psychology professor Richard Eibach was reported last year in the* Washington Post *as having found that in judging racial progress, white people and black ones tend to use different yardsticks. Whites use the yardstick of how far we have come from the nation we used to be. Blacks use the yardstick of how far we have yet to go to be the nation we ought to be.*[1]

Obama Receives the Nobel Peace Prize

Obama was awarded the Nobel Peace Prize in October 2009, less than one year after taking office, which surprised many people. In explaining the choice, the Nobel committee said, "Only very rarely has a person to the same extent as Obama captured the world's attention and given its people hope for a better future."[2]

Pitts added that neither yardstick is complete. Both sides of the story are necessary to get a complete picture of race relations in the United States. In national polls since the early days of the country— including during the time of legalized slavery, the Jim Crow South, and into the twenty-first century— white Americans tend to view the United States as far less racist than Americans of color see it.

To ignore the patterns of racial inequity is to have only a partial view of the United States. Recognizing that so many Americans of color continue to live in poverty and suffer from either personal or institutional racism is integral to the complete picture of the United States.

BE A WITNESS

One step toward healing is to acknowledge incidents of racism. Understanding an issue is the first step to making a difference in or affecting that issue. One can gain a wider perspective and make a more informed analysis by seeking sources that look at history from alternate points of view. Two examples include Howard Zinn's *People's History of the United States* and, more recently, Ronald Takaki's *A Different Mirror*. Understanding history from many perspectives leads to a more informed understanding of the past, which can inform and direct future choices.

Talking about race is also important. Simply not mentioning race and the differences between people will not resolve the issue. In other words, being color-blind is not a solution. In 2006, Birgitte Vittrup of the Children's Research Lab at the University of Texas studied the effects of multicultural children's videos on children's racial attitudes. In conducting the study, some

Progressive Princesses

Movies and television can have a great influence on viewers—both positive and negative. They can teach viewers about other perspectives and cultures, but they can also perpetuate stereotypes. One challenge viewers face is to be aware of characters that embody a popular stereotype or inaccurate ideas of racial or ethnic groups or genders.

The creations of Disney have entertained viewers for decades. They have also presented viewers with particular images. For instance, most princesses in Disney stories have been white. Only four princesses in Disney's history of storytelling have been of color. The first was Jasmine, who appeared in *Aladdin* in 1992. While it was a breakthrough that she hailed from somewhere in the Middle East, Jasmine was relatively ethnically ambiguous and notably lighter skinned than the movie's Arabic villains.

Pocahontas, a Native American, was depicted in a film by the same name in 1995. Three years later, the Chinese heroine Mulan was the title character in the film *Mulan*. In 2009, audiences witnessed the debut of Disney's first African-American princess, Tiana, in *The Princess and the Frog*. In an attempt to create a more accurate picture of her beauty, the creative team reportedly consulted with experts, including Oprah Winfrey and the NAACP.

families dropped out when asked to discuss race. "We don't want to have these conversations with our child. We don't want to point out skin color," two families explained to the researcher.[3] Vittrup found that many white parents had never talked to their children about race. In addition, rather than discuss race, many parents simply explained to their children that everyone is equal.

But this practice did not effectively prevent racism. Vittrup discovered that racial attitudes prevailed even with color-blind parenting. She also concluded that discussing race had a positive impact on racial attitudes. Children in the few families with parents who did discuss race showed dramatic changes in racial attitude in only one week.

Cyberbullies

The National Crime Prevention Council finds that cyberbullying, the use of technology to bully, is increasingly common among teens. Like traditional bullies, cyberbullies—and their victims—come in every color. Bullying incidents can often involve racism. Technology users should protect themselves and their friends by refusing to pass on any bullying, racist, or derogatory e-mails or texts.

Words and Actions

Transcending racism may never be totally possible; there will always be people who hate and people who fear the differences between groups. But education can lead to positive changes in words and actions, which can be a positive example for others.

Thousands listened with hope to a speech delivered by President Obama during the "We Are One: Opening Inaugural Celebration" at the Lincoln Memorial in Washington on January 18, 2009.

The past cannot be changed, and modifying the larger problem of institutional racism requires many people. It also requires action, not only on higher levels, where laws and policies are made, but at lower levels, where voters decide on the people who make legislation and sometimes on the legislation itself.

Rock the Vote encourages young people to use their power to vote. Voting gives citizens a voice. The organization noted of today's young voters,

> *Already, the Millennial Generation is changing the face of politics. Forty-four million strong, we are the largest generation in history and represent more than one-fifth of the electorate. We are also the most diverse generation. Sixty-one percent of Millennials identify as White, while 17% are Hispanic, 15% are Black and 4% are Asian.*[4]

This group has already made history by participating in the election that resulted in the first African-American president.

But those who are not old enough to vote are not without power. Speaking out about racist incidents is one way to help. Recognizing and changing common racial stereotypes is another way to work against racism. Fighting for a cause is also an option. Just as young people during the 1960s fought for civil rights, so, too, can youth today. Advances in technology have made connecting with a cause easier than ever.

President Obama and others emphasize the necessity of working together for the good of all. Working together means differences are not barriers, but rather avenues for understanding, learning, and growing.

Since its earliest days, the United States has been the most diverse nation in the world. Americans depend on and are defined by their diversity. Working together, they can each draw on unique perspectives to create a more equitable and vibrant community.

MOVING FORWARD

The United States has made progress toward ending racism. Still, hate crimes continue and are increasing. And racial disparity remains an issue in core areas, including education, health care, and housing.

Each individual has a story to tell. Race may be part of the story, but it

"Isn't that cool the way you set out to change the world and you end up changing your own life. You want to make the world a better place and you make your world a better place. You start out facing so much resistance and lack of respect and condescension and if you stick to it eventually that transforms into sisterhood, camaraderie, respect and appreciation."[5]

—Ani DiFranco, musician, singer, songwriter, activist, speaking at a National Organization for Women Conference, 2006

"On this day, we gather because we have chosen hope over fear, unity of purpose over conflict and discord."[6]

—*President Barack Obama, inaugural address, January 2009*

is not the whole story. Racism in the United States may never completely end, but Americans can recognize and remove its imprint in their laws, services, politics, and in their hearts and minds. The United States can aim to overcome racism and the many ways it divides and hurts individuals and communities while embracing race and the variety of cultures and experiences it comprises.

Two citizens responded with tears of joy when Obama took the oath of office in 2009. Their reaction mirrored millions of Americans.

TIMELINE

1607	1619	1705
The English arrive in North America and settle land occupied by Native Americans.	The first Africans arrive in North American colonies to work for landowners as indentured servants.	Virginia passes a law to define race.

1882	1896	1922
The Chinese Exclusion Act forbids Chinese from entering the United States and becoming US citizens.	The US Supreme Court's ruling in *Plessy v. Ferguson* establishes a separate but equal policy that segregates public facilities in the South.	In *Ozawa v. United States*, the Supreme Court declares Japanese ineligible for US citizenship because they are not white.

1776

The Declaration of Independence is signed and adopted, but its freedoms are not extended to all individuals in the United States.

1790

The Naturalization Act of 1790 reserves citizenship for whites.

1838–1839

During the Trail of Tears, 15,000 Cherokees are forced to march to new land in Oklahoma. Four thousand die during the journey.

1923

In *United States v. Bhagat Singh Thind*, the Supreme Court declares Asian Indians ineligible for US citizenship because they are not white.

1924

The Immigration Act of 1924 limits the number of immigrants who can enter the United States.

1942–1945

The US government interns more than 100,000 Japanese Americans.

TIMELINE

1954

The Supreme Court's ruling in *Brown v. Board of Education* ends legalized school segregation.

1955

Rosa Parks refuses to give up her seat on a segregated bus. Her action fuels the civil rights movement.

1963

In August, Martin Luther King Jr. leads a march on Washington DC for civil rights.

1980

A People's History of the United States presents the first history from the point of view of those who had been exploited or discriminated against.

1988

On August 10, the US Congress passes the Civil Liberties Act to apologize to Japanese Americans for their internment during World War II.

1990

The Hate Crimes Statistics Act is passed. The federal government begins collecting data on hate crimes.

1964	1965	1972
On July 2, the Civil Rights Act is signed into law, prohibiting discrimination based on race as well as color, ethnicity, and religion.	The Voting Rights Act protects African Americans' rights to vote; the Immigration and Nationality Act ends immigration quotas.	The Equal Employment Opportunities Act is passed and signed into law.

1992	2005	2008
Citizens riot in Los Angeles, California, in response to the outcome of the Rodney King trial and years of discrimination.	The devastation in New Orleans, Louisiana, caused by Hurricane Katrina highlights the issue of race and poverty.	In November, Barack Obama becomes the first African American elected president of the United States.

ESSENTIAL FACTS

AT ISSUE

❖ The effects of racism in the United States include a disparity in resources necessary to meet the basic needs for survival, including education, employment, health care, and housing.

❖ Schools attended primarily by students of color are more likely than white schools to be in areas of poverty.

❖ Most white students have little contact with students of color, except in the South and the Southwest.

❖ At the end of 2008, minorities were considerably more likely than whites to experience unemployment.

❖ Hate crimes occur every year, including more than 9,500 in 2008, 51 percent of which were racially motivated.

❖ Ignoring race does not end racism.

CRITICAL DATES

1619

Africans were brought to the Virginia Colony as indentured servants.

1838–1839

The US government forced 15,000 members of the Cherokee nation to move to an area in what is now Oklahoma.

1865

Slavery was abolished in the United States.

1882

The Chinese Exclusion Act was the first law to exclude immigration based on one's nationality. Similar laws followed.

1896

Plessy v. Ferguson legalized the segregation already established in much of the South and led to increased separation of and disparity between races.

1942–1945

Following Japan's attack on Pearl Harbor, Hawaii, the US government interned more than 100,000 Japanese Americans.

1954

The Supreme Court's ruling in *Brown v. Board of Education* ended segregation in schools and led to integration of all public facilities.

1950s and 1960s

Civil rights activists fought for integrated facilities and equal rights for all.

1964

The Civil Rights Amendment to the US Constitution extended civil rights to all US citizens.

1970s–first decade of 2000

Many people of color rose to great success in a variety of fields. But for many, racial inequity persisted in areas such as education, criminal justice, health care, and housing.

2005

The destruction caused by Hurricane Katrina in New Orleans, Louisiana, highlighted the disparity of the races when the vast majority of those stranded in the city were poor African Americans.

2008

Barack Obama became the first African American elected president of the United States.

Quotes

"Psychology professor Richard Eibach was reported last year in the *Washington Post* as having found that in judging racial progress, white people and black ones tend to use different yardsticks. Whites use the yardstick of how far we have come from the nation we used to be. Blacks use the yardstick of how far we have yet to go to be the nation we ought to be."—*Leonard Pitts Jr., professor and activist, 2009*

GLOSSARY

activist
  A person who supports and is a vigorous advocate for a specific cause.

boycott
  To engage in a group effort to abstain from dealings with a business or organization, usually to gain attention for a cause.

civil liberties
  The freedom to exercise rights, such as free speech, and to gather or assemble.

civil rights
  Rights to personal liberty, established by the Thirteenth and Fourteenth Amendments to the US Constitution.

civil rights movement
  Social movement begun in the 1950s in the United States to end discrimination against and extend full legal, social, and economic equality to African Americans.

desegregation
  To eliminate separation by race or ethnic group.

discrimination
  Treatment or judgment of an individual or group, either for or against, based on being part of an ethnic or racial group.

disparity
  A significant difference between two things.

diversity
  The inclusion of a variety of ethnic, racial, and gender-based groups.

inequity
  Injustice or unfairness.

integration
  The act of incorporating individuals as equals into a society or institution.

justice
> Equality, fairness, and equal rights for all citizens regardless of racial or ethnic group.

Latino
> A person from Latin-American or Hispanic heritage living in the United States.

lynching
> To kill by mob, usually by hanging, without order of the law.

prejudice
> Irrational hostility toward a person or group based on supposed characteristics.

protest
> The public expression of disagreement or disapproval with a policy or practice.

segregation
> The separation of individuals based on some characteristic, such as race, class, ethnicity, or sex.

white supremacist
> A person who believes in the superiority of the white race over all others.

ADDITIONAL RESOURCES

SELECTED BIBLIOGRAPHY

Ifill, Gwen. *The Breakthrough: Politics and Race in the Age of Obama*. New York: Doubleday, 2009. Print.

Immell, Myra H., ed. *Ethnic Violence*. San Diego: Greenhaven, 2000. Print.

Packard, Jerrold M. *American Nightmare: The History of Jim Crow*. New York: St. Martin's, 2002. Print.

Pincus, Fred L. *Reverse Discrimination: Dismantling the Myth*. Boulder, CO: Reinner, 2003. Print.

Takaki, Ronald. *A Different Mirror: A History of Multicultural America*. Boston: Little, 2008. Print.

Wise, Tim. *Between Barack and a Hard Place: Racism and White Denial in the Age of Obama*. San Francisco: City Lights, 2009. Print.

FURTHER READINGS

Desetta, Al, ed. *The Courage to Be Yourself: True Stories by Teens About Cliques, Conflicts, and Overcoming Peer Pressure*. Minneapolis, MN: Free Spirit, 2005. Print.

Obama, Barack. *Dreams from My Father: A Story of Race and Inheritance*. New York: Three Rivers, 2004. Print.

Zinn, Howard, and Rebecca Stefoff. *A Young People's History of the United States. Volume 1: Columbus to the Spanish-American War*. New York: Seven Stories, 2007. Print.

Zinn, Howard, and Rebecca Stefoff. *A Young People's History of the United States. Volume 2: Class Struggle to the War on Terror*. New York: Seven Stories, 2007. Print.

Web Links

To learn more about racism in the United States, visit ABDO Publishing Company online at **www.abdopublishing.com**. Web sites about racism are featured on our Book Links page. These links are routinely monitored and updated to provide the most current information available.

For More Information

For more information on this subject, contact or visit the following organizations.

Civil Rights Memorial
400 Washington Avenue, Montgomery, AL 36104
334-956-8439
www.splcenter.org/civil-rights-memorial
The memorial honors the people who died in the fight for civil rights during the 1950s and 1960s and records the history of the struggle.

The Museum of Tolerance, Los Angeles, California
9786 West Pico Boulevard, Los Angeles, CA 90035-4720
310-553-8403
www.museumoftolerance.com
Interactive exhibits invite viewers to question bias, explore incidents of discrimination and racism, and find ways to live together in peace.

National Association for the Advancement of Colored People
4805 Mt. Hope Drive, Baltimore, MD 21215
410-580-5777
www.naacp.org
The NAACP fights for equal rights of all people in the United States, regardless of race.

SOURCE NOTES

Chapter 1. A City in Flames
1. Louis Menand. "Notable Quotables." *New Yorker*. Condé Nast Digital, 19 Feb. 2007. Web. 25 Oct. 2010.
2. Frances Fox Piven and Richard Clowards. *Poor People's Movements: Why They Succeed, How They Fail*. New York: Random House, 1977. Print. 206.

Chapter 2. Racism in the United States
1. Howard Zinn. *A People's History of the United States: 1492–Present*. New York: Harper, 1980. Print. 1.
2. Ibid.
3. "One Drop Rule." *Encyclopedia of Arkansas History and Culture, Butler Center for Arkansas Studies*. Central Arkansas Library System, 15 July 2009. Web. 25 Oct. 2010.
4. Takaki. *Double Victory: A Multicultural History of America in World War II*. Boston, MA: Back Bay, 2001. Print. 24.
5. "Historical Documents: Civil Liberties Act of 1988." *PBS.org: Children of the Camps*. Satsuki Ina, 1999. Web. 25 Oct. 2010.

Chapter 3. A Decade of Change
1. "About Brown v. Board." *BrownvBoard.org*. Brown Foundation for Educational Equity, Excellence and Research, 11 Apr. 2004. Web. 25 Oct. 2010.
2. "Martin Luther King: I have a Dream." *American Rhetoric: Top One Hundred Speeches*. American Rhetoric, 2010. Web. 25 Oct. 2010.
3. "By Any Means Necessary." *Malcolm X Quotations*. Malcolm. N.p., n.d. Web. 25 Oct. 2010.
4. Jerrold M. Packard. *American Nightmare: The History of Jim Crow*. New York: St. Martin's, 2002. Print. 268.
5. Ibid. 272.

Chapter 4. Education for All
1. Erica Frankenberg and Chungmei Lee. "Race in American Public Schools: Rapidly Resegregating School Districts." 8 Aug. 2002. *The Civil Rights Project, Harvard University*. The Civil Rights Project, UCLA, 2010. Web. 25 Oct. 2010.
2. Michael E. Ross. "Brown v. Board: The education of a nation." *MSNBC.com*. MSNBC.com, 15 Feb. 2005. Web. 25 Oct. 2010.

3. Tim Wise. *Between Barack and a Hard Place: Racism and White Denial in the Age of Obama*. San Francisco: City Lights, 2009. Print. 49.

4. Linda Darling-Hammond. "Inequality in Teaching and Schooling: How Opportunity Is Rationed to Students of Color in America. *The Right Thing to Do, The Smart Thing to Do*. National Academies, 2001. Web. 12 Nov. 2010.

5. "About Us." *Teach for America*. Teach for America, 2010. Web. 25 Oct. 2010.

6. "*Brown* at 50: King's Dream or *Plessy*'s Nightmare?" *Harvard Graduate School of Education*. President and Fellows of Harvard College, 18 Jan. 2004. Web. 25 Oct. 2010.

7. Ibid.

8. "About CEO." *Center for Equal Opportunity*. Center for Equal Opportunity, 2010. Web. 25 Oct. 2010.

9. Associated Press. "Does affirmative action punish whites?" *MSNBC.com*. MSNBC.com, 28 Apr. 2009. Web. 25 Oct. 2010.

10. Fred L. Pincus. *Reverse Discrimination: Dismantling the Myth*. Boulder, CO: Reinner, 2003. Print. 31.

11. Associated Press. "Does affirmative action punish whites?" *MSNBC.com*. MSNBC.com, 28 Apr. 2009. Web. 25 Oct. 2010.

12. Ibid.

Chapter 5. A Case Study in Disparity

1. Carol Bengle Gilbert. "Lilly Ledbetter Fair Pay Act of 2009 Signed into Law." *Associated Content*. Associated Content, Inc., Yahoo! Finance, and Yahoo! News Network, 2010. Web. 12 Nov. 2010.

2. "In quotes: Bush on Katrina." *BBC News*. BBC, 16 Sept. 2005. Web. 25 Oct. 2010.

3. Amanda Logan and Christian E. Weller. "The State of Minorities: The Recession Issue." *Center for American Progress*. Center for American Progress, 16 Jan. 2009. Web. 25 Oct. 2010.

4. "In quotes: Bush on Katrina." *BBC News*. BBC, 16 Sept. 2005. Web. 25 Oct. 2010.

5. G. William Domhoff. "Wealth, Income, and Power." *Who Rules America?* UC Santa Cruz, Sept. 2010. Web. 12 Nov. 2010.

SOURCE NOTES CONTINUED

Chapter 6. Hate Crimes

1. Carol Marie Cropper. "Town Expresses Sadness And Horror Over Slaying." *New York Times*. New York Times Company, 11 June 1998. Web. 25 Oct. 2010.

2. Stephen J. Whitfield. *A Death in the Delta: The Story of Emmett Till*. New York: Free, 1988. Print. 7.

3. "Hate crimes bill goes to Obama for signature." *CNN Politics. com*. Cable News Network, 23 Oct. 2009. Web. 25 Oct. 2010.

4. "Hate Crime." *Crime in the United States 2004*. Department of Justice, Federal Bureau of Investigation, 2004. Web. 25 Oct. 2010.

5. Ibid.

Chapter 7. Race and the Law

1. Manning Marable. "Racism, Prisons, and the Future of Black America." *Peacework 2000/2001*. Peacework Magazine, n.d. Web. 25 Oct. 2010.

2. Ibid.

3. Bruce Western and Becky Pettit. "Beyond Crime and Punishment: Prisons and Inequality." *Contexts*, 1.3 (2002): 37, 41. Web. 25 Oct. 2010.

4. Elizabeth Rudulph and Harriet Barovick. "DWB: Driving While Black." *Time*. Time Inc., 15 June 1998. Web. 28 Oct. 2010.

5. "Who We Are." *Amnesty International*. N.p., n.d. Web. 25 Oct. 2010.

6. "Threat and Humiliation: Racial Profiling, National Security, and Human Rights in the United States." *Amnesty International USA*. Amnesty International USA, 2010. Web. 12 Nov. 2010.

7. Marian Wright Edelman. "Marian Wright Edelman's Child Watch Column: Promising Models for Reforming Juvenile Justice Systems." *Children's Defense Fund*. Children's Defense Fund, 4 Sept 2009. Web. 25 Oct. 2010.

8. Ibid.

Chapter 8. A Landmark Election
1. Natasha Norton. "Obama Wins in a Landslide." *Election 2004*. UC Berkeley Graduate School of Journalism, 2 Nov. 2004. Web. 25 Oct. 2010.
2. Mary Mitchell. "McCain, Palin turn to risky politics." *Chicago Sun-Times*. Sun-Times Media, 9 Oct. 2008. Web. 25 Oct. 2010.
3. Gwen Ifill. *The Breakthrough: Politics and Race in the Age of Obama*. New York: Doubleday, 2009. Print. 62.
4. Ibid. 55.
5. Ibid.
6. Brian Ross and Rehab El-Buri. "Obama's Pastor: God Damn America, U.S. to Blame for 9/11." *ABC News*. ABC News Internet Ventures, 13 Mar. 2008. Web. 25 Oct. 2010.
7. "Transcript: Barack Obama's Speech on Race." *NPR*. NPR, 18 Mar. 2008. Web. 25 Oct. 2010.
8. "A More Perfect Union." *America.gov*. US Department of State, 11 Jan. 2009. Web. 25 Oct 2010.

Chapter 9. An Ongoing Issue
1. Leonard Pitts Jr. "Commentary: 'Post-racial' America isn't here yet." *CNNPolitics.com*. Cable News Network, 28 Mar. 2009. Web. 25 Oct. 2010.
2. "Obama: Nobel Peace Prize is 'call to action.'" *CNN.com/Europe*. Cable News Network, Turner Broadcasting, 9 Oct. 2009. Web. 25 Oct. 2010.
3. Po Bronson and Ashley Merryman. "See Baby Discriminate." *Newsweek*. Harman Newsweek, 5 Sept. 2009. Web. 25 Oct. 2010.
4. "Who Are Young Voters?" *Rock the Vote*. Rock the Vote, 2010. Web. 25 Oct. 2010.
5. "Quotable Quotes from Speakers and Honorees at the 2006 National NOW Conference and Young Feminist Summit." *National Organization for Women*. National Organization for Women, 2009. Web. 25 Oct. 2010.
6. "Transcript: Barack Obama's Inaugural Address." *New York Times*. New York Times Company, 20 Jan. 2009. Web. 25 Oct. 2010.

INDEX

ABOUT THE AUTHOR

A. M. Buckley is an artist and writer. She has written 14 books for children. A former bilingual elementary schoolteacher, she works as a mentor to new classroom teachers. Buckley has taught students from kindergarten through graduate school. A graduate of the University of California, Berkeley, she enjoys the diversity of California's public schools and universities. Buckley lives in Los Angeles, California.

PHOTO CREDITS